# Beneath Her Silence

## Some Shadows Don't Fade

Yogyasri Mande

BookLeaf Publishing
India | USA | UK

Made with ❤ on the BookLeaf Publishing Platform
www.bookleafpub.in
www.bookleafpub.com

# Dedication

*To the ones who carry storms in silence,*
*who write poems in the dark when no one's watching.*
*And to Sreehitha,Seraphine and Charita,*
*for being the voice beside mine,*
*when mine was too heavy to speak.*

# Preface

They say silence speaks louder than words. But what if that silence holds screams no one hears? What if it remembers the things we try to forget?

When Meher stepped into the gates of her new school, she didn't know she was walking into the heart of a story that had never ended. A photo. A diary. A house that remembers. And a voice that had waited too long in the dark.

This isn't just a story about ghosts—it's about truths we bury, pain we inherit, and the things that follow us when we think we've moved on. It's about friendship and fear, about losing everything just as you start to understand it.

What lies ahead is not just a mystery—it's a haunting. One that lingers long after the final page.

Read with the lights on.

And listen closely to the silence.

Because sometimes, it's the quietest stories that hurt the most.

# Acknowledgements

To the voices that never found their way out,
To the hearts that have been silenced,
To the ones who feel too much but say too little—this is for you.
Thank you, Amma and Nanna, for always letting me find my voice, even in the quietest moments.
To Sreehitha, Sera and Charita, my constant through every whispered fear and unspoken hope—you were the silence that understood.
To the fragments of me that never learnt to speak aloud—you live on these pages.
And to you, the reader, if you find yourself lost in Meher's silence, remember—some stories don't need to be heard to be felt.

This story is my heart.
— *Yogyasri Mande*

# CHAPTER ONE

# The Vanishing

The last time Meher heard her mother's voicc, it was saying her name.

Just once.

Soft, like the hush of wind against an open window.

"Meher."

And then... silence.

That night, the rain tapped gently against the glass. Her mother had promised to come back before dinner—she never broke promises. So Meher waited. She waited until the shadows stretched too long and the rice grew cold on the plates. The front door never opened. Her father sat still at the dining table, staring at the wall like it held answers. And something in Meher's chest cracked quietly, so quietly she didn't even notice the sound of her own voice disappearing.

She hasn't spoken since.

Now, two years later, Meher's world moves without her

sound.

Her school days are a blur of footsteps, books, and people who talk around her but never to her. Teachers smile too much. Classmates avoid her like silence is contagious.

Only two people seem to look her in the eye anymore:

Her father—who looks at her with a guilt he never speaks of.

And her English teacher, Ms. Iqbal—who watches Meher as if she's a riddle waiting to be solved.

That morning, Ms. Iqbal slid a sheet of paper onto Meher's desk.

Not an assignment. Not a test. Just one question, written in looping ink:

**"If you could speak again, what would you say?"**

Meher stared at the words until they blurred.

And for the first time in two years, her fingers itched to answer.

## CHAPTER TWO

# Paper Planes And Broken Things

Meher didn't answer the question.

Not because she didn't want to.

But because she wasn't sure what the truth would sound like anymore.

Her fingers hovered over the edge of the paper all through English class. She folded it once. Then again. Creased it perfectly until the question disappeared beneath sharp corners and silence. And then, just before the bell rang, she flicked it out the open window like a paper plane—like maybe the wind would carry the answer for her.

She didn't look back.

At lunch, Meher sat under the tamarind tree near the back of the school grounds. It was her favorite place. The one spot no one bothered her—where the noise of the world softened into birdsong and distant footsteps. She leaned her head against the bark, let her eyes close for a second too long...

And when she opened them, a girl was standing there.

Not looking at her, exactly.

Just... there.

She had messy hair like she didn't care about mornings, and her eyes were darker than anything Meher had seen. Not cruel. Just tired. Familiar. Like they'd seen things they shouldn't have.

"Is it true?" she asked.

Meher blinked.

Most people didn't talk to her. They talked around her. Or worse—about her.

"That you don't speak?"

She didn't move. Silence had become her skin now—anything else felt like too much.

"I won't tell anyone," she added quickly. "I just... I found this."

She held something out.

Her paper plane.

Unfolded. Flattened. The question now smudged by someone else's fingerprints.

**"If you could speak again, what would you say?"**

Meher looked at her for a long moment.

And for reasons she couldn't explain,

her heart whispered something it hadn't felt in a very

long time:

**Safe.**

## CHAPTER THREE

# Things We Don't Say

Her name was Ananya.

Meher didn't ask. She just told her.

"I'm new here. Just moved last week. My parents think changing schools fixes everything."

She knew that tone—half sarcasm, half sadness. The kind that pretends not to care, but deep down... still does.

Ananya didn't wait for her to reply. She just sat beside her, leaving a respectful distance, like she knew she wouldn't like anyone too close. She didn't ask why she didn't speak again. She didn't press her for answers or pity her in that suffocating way people often did.

She just... sat.

And in that simple silence, something shifted.

Over the next few days, she started showing up more. Sometimes with a book in hand, sometimes just with a

question like,
"Do you think memories lie?"
or
"Do you ever feel like someone's hiding something from you?"
She never answered, but she didn't seem to mind. It was as if she already knew the truth lived somewhere in her eyes, not her mouth.
One day, she brought her a notebook.
"It's blank," she said, placing it in her lap.
"I thought maybe... if it's hard to speak, you could write instead."
Meher stared at it, unsure what scared her more—the idea of sharing, or the risk that someone might actually read what she truly felt.
But that night, for the first time in two years, she opened it.
And wrote just five words on the first page:
**"I think I remember something."**

## CHAPTER FOUR

# The First Crack

The sentence stared back at her all night.

*I think I remember something.*

Meher's handwriting was shaky, like her truth was still deciding whether it wanted to be seen. But the moment the words touched paper, a crack opened somewhere inside her. And with it came a feeling she hadn't felt in a long time—

Fear.

She closed the notebook and shoved it under her bed, heart pounding like she'd said something forbidden.

Because the truth was, Meher hadn't remembered anything clearly in years. That night—*the* night—had always been blurry. Fuzzy shapes. A door slamming. Her mother's voice. Then nothing.

But lately, fragments had been returning.

A silver bracelet.

The smell of sandalwood.

A shadow standing just outside her bedroom window.
She didn't know what any of it meant. But she knew something wasn't right. And her silence… it wasn't just grief anymore. It was protection. From what, she still didn't know.
At school the next day, Ananya noticed.
"You didn't sleep," she said quietly, sliding into her usual seat beside her.
She shook her head once.
She didn't press. Instead, she pulled something out of her bag—a small, old Polaroid camera.
"My dad gave it to me years ago. Says you can capture more than just images with it. You can capture... moments. Feelings."
She paused, then handed it to her. "Take it. Use it when something feels off. Pictures don't lie like memories do."
Meher held the camera in her hands like it was made of glass. It was scratched, worn, but warm.
And for the first time since her mother disappeared, Meher felt something small and terrifying growing in her chest again.
**Hope.**

## CHAPTER FIVE

# The Photograph

The camera sat on her desk all day, untouched.
Meher stared at it like it might blink first—like it might tell her why a lump had settled in her throat the second Ananya handed it to her. She didn't believe in signs. Not really. But this... felt like one.
That night, the power went out.
A summer storm swept across the town with angry winds and a sky stitched with lightning. Meher sat on the edge of her bed, the camera in her lap, her window open just a crack.
That's when she saw it.
A flicker.
A silhouette standing across the street.
Someone was watching the house.
Meher's breath caught.
Her fingers moved before she could think—lifting the Polaroid, snapping a photo through the open window.

The flash lit the night for half a second.

And then—

Gone.

No one.

Nothing.

Just a heartbeat loud in her ears.

Her hands trembled as the photo slid out of the camera.

She watched as it developed slowly, lines and shapes forming in the milky fog.

The result made her stomach twist.

A man.

Partially obscured.

Face unclear.

But unmistakably there.

Not her imagination. Not grief. Not a shadow.

**Someone was watching her.**

She stared at the picture until the edges curled. Then did something she hadn't done in years.

She cried. Not because she was scared.

But because, for the first time... she *wasn't crazy.*

And that meant someone had been lying to her all along.

## CHAPTER SIX

# The Lie In The Lullaby

There was a lullaby her mother used to hum.

Soft. Crooked. A tune that never felt finished.

Meher hadn't heard it in years — not even in her dreams.

Until last night.

The moment she woke up, drenched in sweat, she knew it wasn't imagined. She had heard it. *Hummed, not sung.* Right outside her window, floating through the storm like it belonged to the night.

She checked the Polaroid again that morning. The man in the photo was no longer just a blur to her. Something about the slope of his shoulders, the sharpness of the jawline — it pulled at something deep, buried. Like a memory just out of reach.

And with that, another crack appeared in her silence.

She went to school but didn't hear a word. Not the teachers, not the bell, not even Ananya asking if she was okay.

She wasn't.

At lunch, she finally pulled her aside.

"There's something I need to show you," she whispered, handing her the photo.

Her face turned serious as she stared at it. "When did you take this?"

"Last night."

"And you're sure... this isn't just—?"

"It's real," she said. "And there's something else. I heard... her lullaby."

She blinked. "Your mom's?"

Meher nodded. Her throat was tight, but she managed the words.

"What if she didn't leave?"

"What if someone made her disappear?"

Ananya looked at her like she was seeing her for the first time. Not the silent girl. Not the shattered daughter.

But the girl who might be ready to find the truth.

Even if it broke her all over again.

## CHAPTER SEVEN

# The Room She Left Behind

The door had always been locked.

Her mother's room – left untouched since the day she vanished. It sat like a sealed vault at the end of the hallway, collecting dust and silence.

But that evening, something was different.

The key was in the lock.

Meher stood frozen, her fingers hovering just inches from it. She hadn't seen that key since her father shoved it into a drawer the day after the police stopped looking.

She didn't ask questions then.

She just stopped speaking.

Now, her breath shaky, she turned it.

The door creaked open.

The scent hit her first – faint jasmine and old wood. The kind of smell that carries memory in it. The curtains were drawn. Dust curled in the fading light. Everything was still in place. Her mother's books. Her scarf on the chair. A notebook half-open on the bed.

Meher stepped inside slowly, afraid to disturb something sacred.

Then—footsteps.

"Meher?"

Ananya's voice came from behind, soft but urgent. She peeked through the crack. "You went in?"

Meher nodded.

Ananya joined her, eyes scanning the room. "It's like time stopped in here."

She picked up the notebook. Meher reached for it too, her fingers brushing Ananya's. Inside, page after page was filled with her mother's handwriting – lyrics, letters, some half-crossed out, some angry, some aching.

Then one page stopped them cold.

"*If they find out, it's over.*

*They won't believe me.*

*But Meher will.*"

Ananya looked at her. "What is this?"

Meher didn't speak. Couldn't.

Because for the first time in years, she knew this wasn't just grief.

This was a **trail**.

And her mother had left it for *her*.

## CHAPTER EIGHT

# Echoes Through Paper Walls

The letter haunted her all night.

*"If they find out, it's over.*

*They won't believe me.*

*But Meher will."*

She read it again and again until the words stopped feeling real. Until her mother's voice sounded like her own. Until silence started to scream.

Ananya had copied the note into her phone before they carefully placed the journal back. Neither of them wanted her father to know they'd opened the room. Not yet.

"Do you think your dad ever read this?" Ananya asked quietly.

Meher didn't answer. Because deep down, she knew — **he hadn't**. Or worse, he had... and chose to forget.

The next day, Meher found herself outside the library after school, the journal page burned into her brain. Ananya was beside her, holding a faded school year book they'd borrowed after hours.

"We're looking for anyone who might've known her," Ananya explained. "Teachers, friends. Someone who might have seen something."

They flipped through the pages until they found it — a staff photo from over a decade ago. There she was. Meher's mother. Smiling, but distant. Not like the home videos. Not like how Meher remembered her.

And next to her... a man with his hand on her shoulder.

"Do you know him?" Ananya asked.

Meher stared at the photo. The sharp jawline. The watch. The half-smile.

It was the man from the Polaroid.

The one in the trees that night.

Her heart stuttered.

"We need to find him," Meher whispered.

And for the first time in years, her voice didn't crack when she said it.

## CHAPTER NINE

# The Man Behind The Smile

The name beneath the yearbook photo was **Mr. Rishaan Dutt**.

Former Literature teacher. Left the school abruptly the year Meher's mother disappeared.

No farewell. No explanation.

Ananya leaned back in her chair at the library, scrolling through an old alumni group online. "Nothing on social media. It's like he vanished too."

Meher stared at the photo again. The way his hand rested on her mother's shoulder. Not just friendly. *Familiar*. It made something uneasy settle in her chest.

"What if he was involved?" she whispered.

Ananya didn't answer at first. Then, "What if he was the only one who *tried* to help her?"

Meher looked at her. "Why would she write that note if

someone was helping her?"

Ananya hesitated. "Sometimes help becomes a weapon."

The silence that followed wasn't heavy. It was searching.

Later that night, Meher sat by her window, the Polaroid in one hand and the journal page in the other. The wind rattled the glass. The trees swayed — whispering secrets only she could hear.

And then she saw it.

A figure near the trees. Just standing. Watching.

She blinked.

Gone.

But the cold in her spine stayed.

She wasn't imagining things. Someone was watching her house.

And if it *was* Rishaan Dutt...

Then he didn't vanish.

He was **waiting**.

## CHAPTER TEN

# His Name In The Dark

The next day, Meher didn't go to school.

She told her father she had a stomach ache. He didn't ask further – he rarely did anymore.

But really, she needed quiet.

She needed to think.

She pulled out everything – the Polaroid, the journal copy, the yearbook photo. She lined them up on her floor like puzzle pieces that refused to fit.

Then came a knock at her window.

She startled.

It was Ananya, crouching outside with her phone held up. "Come down," she mouthed.

They met by the park, beneath the old swing set where they used to play as kids. Ananya handed Meher her phone. An article was open. Faded and barely archived.

**"Local Teacher Under Investigation for Unprofessional Conduct — Rishaan Dutt Resigns Amid Controversy."**

No charges. Just whispers.

"She was trying to report him," Meher said quietly, connecting the dots.

Ananya nodded. "And no one believed her. So she wrote to you instead."

Meher swallowed hard. Her mother's final cry for help wasn't some poetic mystery — it was a **warning**.

And no one had listened.

Except her.

Back at home, she found herself standing at the door to the study — her father's space. She shouldn't have gone in. But something pulled her.

There, inside an old drawer, she found a folder.

Her mother's name on it.

She opened it slowly.

Inside were copies of letters.

Letters her mother had written to the school board. To the police. To her husband.

**Begging** for someone to believe her.

All dated weeks before she disappeared.

And on the last letter — scrawled in her father's handwriting:

"Let it go. It's not worth what it'll cost."

The words sliced through her like ice.

She backed away.

Her father had known.
He had known.

## CHAPTER ELEVEN

# Whispers Under The Floorboards

She didn’t speak to her father for two days.

But silence wasn't new in their house — it had lived there long before her mother vanished.

The difference now? Meher was finally **listening** to it.

That night, something felt *off*. The air wasn’t just cold — it was charged. As if the walls were holding their breath, waiting.

The hallway lights flickered once. Then again.

She pulled her hoodie tighter, heart thudding with every creak the house made.

Sleep was impossible. Her mother’s handwriting haunted her. Those letters, that warning. Her father’s cold scrawl across the final page.

**“Let it go. It’s not worth what it’ll cost.”**

What had it cost?

She needed answers. And something — some quiet pull — told her they were hidden **upstairs**.

The attic.

It had always been locked. Off-limits. The one room her father never touched.

But tonight, the key sat in the kitchen drawer like it had been waiting.

The attic door groaned as she turned the key.

She hesitated.

The smell hit her first — stale air mixed with **metal**, and something else.

Like *something had been buried and forgotten.*

Her phone light barely cut through the dark. Dust danced in thick beams. Furniture lay like abandoned corpses under sheets. Broken mirrors leaned against peeling walls.

But in the farthest corner, under a table, was a **red thread**.

Thin. Faded. Familiar.

Meher's breath caught.

Her mother wore one just like it. Every day. On her left wrist.

She stepped closer, kneeling. As her fingers touched the thread—

**Knock.**

She froze.

It came from **beneath the floorboards**.

She didn't move.

**Knock.**

Louder this time. Three slow, hollow thuds.

She turned, phone light shaking. "H-Hello?"

Silence.

Then a whisper.

She couldn't make out the words, but it was there.

**Someone was whispering.**

From under her feet.

She stepped back, wood creaking beneath her.

Her flashlight flickered.

A **chill ran through her**, deep and unnatural — like something had just crawled over her skin.

She backed toward the door. Her phone buzzed.

One new message.

From a **blocked number**.

It simply read:

"You opened it. She's not the only one who won't come back."

Her blood ran cold.

The attic door slammed shut behind her.

## CHAPTER TWELVE

# What The Walls Remember

The attic door wouldn't open.

Meher banged against it, her breaths ragged, eyes wild in the dim light.

"Open up!" she hissed, her voice breaking the silence for the first time in hours.

Then—click.

It creaked open by itself.

No wind.

No footsteps.

Just that click.

She stumbled down the stairs, her phone clutched tight in her hand, the red thread now wound around her fingers like a tether.

The house was too quiet.

Even the clock in the hall — the one that always ticked —

had stopped.

**2:13 AM.**

She blinked.

That wasn't the time before.

The second she entered her room, her closet door creaked open an inch.

Just enough.

To let something breathe.

She didn't sleep. She sat by the window till dawn, watching shadows crawl across her floor like they had minds of their own.

—

In the morning, she tried telling her father.

He looked at her.

And smiled.

That cold, practiced smile that never reached his eyes.

"Stop digging, Meher. There are things in this house that should stay buried."

And then he walked away.

She stood frozen, mouth open.

He **knew**.

He knew what was in the attic. Maybe he even put it there.

Was he hiding something?

Or **someone**?

—

That evening, Meher followed a trail of ash.

It began in the hallway and ended in her mother's old studio.

Everything was gone. Covered in white cloth.

Except the mirror.

It was cracked.

But only one reflection stared back.

**Hers.**

Not the room. Not the table behind her.

Just her.

Until she blinked.

And then **her mother** was in the frame. Standing behind her.

No eyes. Just tears of black ink.

Meher turned around.

No one.

She looked back.

The mirror was whole.

And empty.

Her phone buzzed again.

"You're close. But so is she."

Who was *she*?

And what did they mean by **close**?

Meher didn't know yet, but something inside her was breaking open — memories she had buried, emotions she didn't understand, and a grief so sharp it tasted like blood.

She clutched the red thread tighter.

Whatever this was… it had only just begun.

## CHAPTER THIRTEEN

# The Whispers In The Walls

Meher didn't tell anyone about the mirror. Or the figure she saw. She couldn't. Every time she tried, the words tangled on her tongue like cobwebs. Like something was stopping her.

That night, she didn't sleep in her room.

She curled up on the living room couch, facing the doorway. Her fingers still wore the red thread like a bandage—maybe even a shield. The silence wasn't peaceful anymore. It was heavy. Loaded. Like the house was breathing with her. Or against her.

At exactly 3:12 AM, the lights flickered.

And then they died.

She didn't move.

The sound started again. That same scraping. From the attic. From the walls. From underneath the floorboards.

But this time... it was closer.
A soft humming drifted through the dark.
A lullaby.
One Meher hadn't heard since she was a child. Her mother used to sing it when storms would rattle their windows. But her mother was gone.
Wasn't she?
Meher's body trembled. She stood up slowly, legs stiff with fear, and followed the sound. Each step felt like walking through water. As she neared the base of the staircase, she saw something scrawled on the wall in charcoal-gray strokes.
**"She never left. But neither did her pain."**
The humming stopped.
The hallway was suddenly colder.
She turned—and standing at the end of it was a woman in a white saree. Not glowing. Not ghostly. Just *wrong*.
Her head tilted. Her hair dripping wet. Her face blurry. Like someone had tried to erase her.
Meher's breath caught in her throat.
The woman raised a hand. Not to wave. To point.
At Meher.
And then she disappeared.
No sound. No movement. Just gone.
Meher fell to her knees. Her heart was racing, but her body felt numb. She knew now—this wasn't just a haunted house. This was a house of grief, of memories

trapped in walls that never forgot, of screams swallowed by silence.

And maybe, just maybe... the silence had been trying to speak all along.

## CHAPTER FOURTEEN

# The Attic Door

The next morning, Meher didn't mention the woman. Not to her father. Not to Ananya. What would she even say? That she saw her dead mother standing in the hallway pointing at her?

Instead, she sat at the breakfast table, silent. Numb. Every tick of the clock sounded like a countdown. To what, she didn't know.

Ananya noticed. "You didn't sleep," she whispered. "Did you see something again?"

Meher blinked slowly. "I don't know. I think... I think the house is trying to tell me something."

Ananya didn't laugh this time. She didn't even look surprised. She just said, "Then maybe you should listen."

That evening, the attic door opened by itself.

No wind. No tremor. No reason.

Meher had walked past it a hundred times since moving back. But this time, it was open. Just a crack. Enough to see the dust swirl in the air like ash. Enough to hear the faintest whisper.

**"Come up."**

She didn't want to. Every part of her screamed to turn away, to run, to shut herself in a room and wait for the sun. But something stronger pulled her forward. Not curiosity. Not courage.

Desperation.

The wooden stairs creaked beneath her feet. The darkness above felt endless, like the attic wasn't part of the house anymore — but a different world. One stitched from shadows and memories and things long forgotten.

She reached the top.

At first, there was nothing. Just trunks. Dust. Cobwebs that hung like torn lace.

And then her foot hit something hard.

She looked down.

A small wooden music box.

She picked it up, hands shaking, and opened the lid.

It played a tune she hadn't heard in ten years.

Her mother's lullaby.

But the tune was off. Slowed. Warped.

And then something spilled out from beneath the velvet lining — a folded note, yellowed with time.

Meher opened it.

It wasn't written in her mother's handwriting. It was jagged, rushed. Almost panicked.

**"She's not dead. She's trapped. And they're watching you now."**

Her fingers trembled. The air around her thickened. She heard footsteps — slow, heavy ones — coming up the attic stairs.

But no one was there.

And yet... someone was breathing just behind her.

## CHAPTER FIFTEEN

# The Things That Breathe

Meher spun around, but the attic was empty.

No footsteps. No person. Just the walls pressing closer, the old wood groaning as if the house itself was trying to speak. The air was icy, not like a draft – but like something cold had just passed through her.

She clutched the note to her chest and stumbled down the attic stairs, her breath shallow, her fingers twitching as though they didn't belong to her anymore.

Downstairs, Ananya looked up. "You're pale."

Meher couldn't speak. She just handed her the note.

Ananya read it slowly. And her lips parted. "Who wrote this?"

"I don't know," Meher whispered. "But it was in a music box. My mom's lullaby was inside. The song was wrong... distorted. And I... I felt like someone was there

with me."
They both sat in silence, the kind that doesn't comfort — the kind that watches.
That night, Meher couldn't sleep. Every creak of the house felt alive. Every shadow had weight. And when the clock struck 3 a.m., she heard it again.
Breathing.
Not outside her room. Not in the hallway.
Inside.
She turned on the light.
No one.
But her window, which had been locked for years, was open just an inch.
She approached it slowly. Cold air leaked through like something exhaling from the other side.
That's when she saw it.
Written in condensation on the glass — five words.
**"You're not supposed to remember."**
Meher stumbled back, heart pounding so hard she could feel it in her throat. She grabbed her phone, hands shaking, and texted Ananya:
**Meher:** *They know I found the note.*
**Ananya:** *Get out of that house.*
But where would she go? Every memory, every clue, every lie was tied to this place. If her mother wasn't dead... if she was *trapped*... then this house wasn't just haunted.

It was hiding someone.
Or something.

## CHAPTER SIXTEEN

# Pages That Shouldn't Exist

The morning felt like a lie. Sunlight spilled through the windows as if it belonged, but Meher knew better now. The warmth didn't reach her bones.

After last night, nothing did.

She found the diary in a place no one should've looked — wedged behind the false panel of her father's study bookshelf. It was bound in cracked leather, stained and stitched as though someone had tried to keep it alive.

She didn't recognize the handwriting at first.

But she knew the signature.

**Saanvi Kapoor.**

Her mother.

Meher's heart stopped. Her hands trembled as she turned the first page. Inside was a date — *a week before her mother vanished.*

*"He doesn't know I'm writing this. But I can't stay silent anymore. Meher is hearing things. Seeing things I've seen before. And the house... it changes at night."*

The air shifted around her. She swallowed.

Page after page, her mother wrote of strange events — footsteps when no one was home, doors that closed on their own, Meher waking up with scratches she couldn't explain. And something worse...

*"There's a room no one remembers. But Meher sleepwalks to it. She speaks in her sleep. Things that aren't hers. Things that scare even me."*

Meher dropped the book, her chest heaving. Her fingers were ice.

This wasn't just grief. This was a trail — a voice reaching from the past, trying to tell her something.

Ananya arrived fifteen minutes later. She barely said a word as Meher shoved the diary into her hands.

Ananya skimmed it, her expression darkening. "Your mom knew. She *knew* something was happening to you."

"I need to find the room," Meher said. "The one that doesn't exist."

Ananya looked at her. "You know how that sounds, right?"

Meher didn't answer. Her eyes were fixed on the staircase. And somewhere above them — just beyond the reach of memory — was a door.

A door not marked on any map.

Not remembered by anyone living.

But it remembered *her.*

And tonight, she'd open it.

Even if it meant she wouldn't be able to close it again.

## CHAPTER SEVENTEEN

# The Door That Remembers

It was 2:14 a.m. when Meher opened her eyes – not because she woke up, but because something wanted her to.

The silence wasn't silent anymore.

There was humming. Faint, off-key, like a nursery rhyme long forgotten. The sound floated through the air vents, and though her bedroom door was closed, the humming felt like it was inside her walls.

Inside her.

She slipped out of bed without switching on the light. Even in the dark, she moved like she knew where to go. Maybe some part of her did. The diary had mentioned sleepwalking. Maybe her body remembered more than her mind ever would.

She crossed the hallway. At the end of it, beside the

dusty attic ladder, there was an unremarkable stretch of wall.

She stared at it.

Nothing. Just paint and plaster.

Until the humming stopped.

And the doorknob appeared.

It didn't *fade in*. It didn't *slide out*. It just — *was*, suddenly. Like it had always been there and Meher had been the blind one.

The knob was ice. She turned it.

Behind the door was a staircase spiraling *downward*. Not up, like an attic. Down. Below a house that had no basement.

She should've turned back.

But the air smelled like her mother's scarf. Faint sandalwood and lemon soap.

So she descended.

The staircase creaked, and the walls whispered things she didn't understand. She didn't bring her phone. She didn't bring Ananya. It felt like a rule — like *this* was something she had to do alone.

At the bottom, she found it.

A room lined with mirrors.

But none of the reflections were hers.

Each mirror showed a different version of the room — flickering like static. In one, she saw herself holding the diary and crying. In another, she saw her mother, eyes wide and screaming, reaching out — before something *dragged her out of frame.*

Meher stumbled backward.

The lights in the mirrors flickered.

One reflection didn't move at all.

She stepped closer.

It wasn't her reflection.

It was... another girl.

Same eyes. Same lips.

But colder.

Emotionless.

And then it smiled.

Not kindly.

Not sadly.

But like it *knew something she didn't.*

The mirror cracked.

Meher screamed, but no sound left her mouth. Her reflection didn't scream. It just *watched*, tilting its head slowly, as if wondering how long Meher would survive down here.

And then Meher noticed — on the floor, under one of the mirrors — a piece of cloth.

Her mother's scarf.

Stained.

Torn.

Left behind like a warning.

## CHAPTER EIGHTEEN

# Her Eyes Were Different

Meher didn't remember walking back up the stairs.

She just remembered the cold.

How it clung to her like wet skin, how it filled her lungs, how the house seemed to shift as she passed through it—walls tighter, shadows longer. Like it was watching her now.

The scarf was still in her hand.

She clutched it like it was the only real thing left in the world. The mirrors... the girl with her face... the scream that never left her throat — all of it pressed against her mind like fogged glass.

The door was gone when she turned around.

Just blank wall again.

The hallway silent. Still.

As if none of it ever happened.

She didn't sleep. She didn't cry. She just waited for morning.

When Ananya arrived, Meher nearly threw herself into her arms. But something made her pause.

Ananya was smiling.

Too easily.

Too early.

"Hey," she said, placing a hand on Meher's shoulder. "You okay? You look like you haven't slept in a week."

Meher opened her mouth to answer — and stopped.

Ananya's eyes weren't the same.

Something was different. Off. As if someone had painted her face too perfectly. As if her warmth had been *practiced.*

"Meher?" she asked again, tilting her head.

The exact way the *reflection* had tilted its head in the mirror.

Meher took a step back.

"I found something," she said slowly, testing her.

"Oh?" Ananya blinked. "What did you find?"

"Something underground," Meher said. "A room. With mirrors."

Ananya didn't move.

Didn't ask questions.

Didn't even look surprised.

She just said, "You went alone?"

Meher's heart dropped.

She hadn't told her she went alone.

"I didn't say that," Meher whispered.

Ananya's smile faded.

Just slightly.

Meher clenched the scarf tighter in her fist. Her voice was thin, shaking. "You were the only person I trusted."

Ananya didn't answer. She looked at the scarf. "Where did you get that?"

"You know where."

Ananya's expression shifted then — not angry. Not confused. Just... hollow. Like she stopped pretending.

And in a voice too calm, she said:

**"You weren't supposed to go there yet."**

# CHAPTER NINETEEN

# The Girl Who Wasn't Ananya

Meher didn't move.

Neither did Ananya.

The silence between them wasn't normal. It wasn't the quiet you fall into with friends. It was the kind of silence that presses into your bones – cold, watchful, listening.

"You weren't supposed to go there yet."

The words echoed louder than they should have. Like the house was holding onto them, refusing to let them fade.

Meher stepped back.

Ananya stepped forward.

Same rhythm. Opposite intent.

"I want to show you something," Ananya said. Her voice was gentle, but it didn't belong in the room. It felt... rehearsed. Hollow. The kind of voice that would hum a lullaby while locking the door behind you.

"No," Meher breathed.

But her legs didn't run. They never did, not in this house.

Ananya — or whatever she was — reached out. Meher flinched back.

That hand was too cold.

Too pale.

Too still.

"I saw you," Meher whispered, "in the mirror."

Ananya froze.

The air in the room seemed to darken.

There was no more smile. No more warmth.

"You're not her," Meher said, voice cracking. "You're not even close."

The girl tilted her head again — and this time, the movement was *wrong*. Like a puppet. Too smooth. Too slow.

Then the voice changed.

Not fully — just enough to make Meher's stomach turn.

**"Neither are you."**

Meher's throat closed.

"What?"

The girl — the thing — stepped closer.

"You don't remember, do you?" it whispered. "What you saw. What you did."

Meher's memories raced. The night her mother disappeared. The night that had been locked inside her like a secret too dark to touch.

“You buried it,” the girl said. “Because you couldn’t live with it.”

Something cracked inside Meher’s chest.

“No,” she gasped. “I didn’t— I was a kid—”

“You opened the door,” the thing said, now inches from her face. “You let it in.”

Suddenly, Meher’s hands were trembling.

Not from fear — from recognition.

She had seen that smile before.

Not on her mother. Not on Ananya.

But in the mirror.

**On herself.**

## CHAPTER TWENTY

# THE MEMORY MEANT TO STAY BURIED

Meher ran.

Down the hallway, past the old clock that had stopped at 3:17 long ago, past the cracked photo of her family—only now she noticed, her mother's eyes were scratched out.

She didn't remember that.

Or did she?

The door at the end of the hall creaked open. She hadn't touched it. Hadn't even gone near it.

Yet it opened.

It always did.

Beyond it was the old guest room — the one her mother had kept locked. Always locked.

Except for that one night.
She shouldn't go in.
She went in.
The floor groaned beneath her bare feet, but it wasn't the sound of wood — it was heavier, like a breath held too long. Her eyes scanned the room, and everything felt... untouched. Like it was waiting.
There was a trunk in the corner.
It hadn't been there before.
She knelt in front of it, fingers trembling. The lock had already been broken. She didn't remember breaking it. But her hands knew how to open it. Like they had done it before.
Inside were photographs.
A whole stack.
Each one of Meher.
Each one... different.
Her face was always the same.
But in every photo — there was no reflection in her eyes.
Just black.
She flipped them faster, chest tightening. Then, beneath the photos, a tape recorder.
She pressed play.
A child's voice echoed from the machine. Her voice.
*"Mommy, there's a girl in my mirror."*
Her breath caught.
The recording continued.

*"She said if I don't let her out, she'll take you instead."*

Click.

The tape stopped.

Meher staggered back, falling onto the floor. Her eyes burned, her lungs wouldn't expand. She couldn't cry — couldn't even scream.

Because now she remembered.

Her mother hadn't disappeared.

Meher had given her away.

She had traded her.

She had *invited* the girl in.

## CHAPTER TWENTY ONE

# The Mirror Remembers

She hadn't slept.

Not because she couldn't – but because she was afraid that if she closed her eyes, *the girl* would be waiting when she opened them.

The mirror in her room had always been there. Framed in peeling white, shaped like an oval tear. She remembered brushing her hair in front of it. Talking to it when she was little. Playing pretend.

Except... what if it wasn't pretend?

What if it had always listened?

The tape played in her mind on loop: *"She said if I don't let her out, she'll take you instead."*

The door to her room creaked open by itself.

She didn't flinch.

She knew it was time.

Her feet moved before her mind could stop them. She stood in front of the mirror.
The lights flickered.
Once.
Twice.
And then—darkness.
But the mirror glowed faintly. The glass shimmered. A slow fog spread across it from the inside, like a breath on winter glass.
Words began appearing.
Not drawn.
**Scratched.**
*"I'm still here."*
Meher stepped back, pulse slamming in her throat.
*"You let me in. You can't lock me out now."*
"No," she whispered.
Her voice trembled — the first sound she had spoken aloud in days.
The mirror trembled too.
And then she saw her.
Not a reflection.
But a girl, just like her.
Exactly like her.
Except for the eyes.
Completely black.
Empty.
The girl raised a finger. Pointed to Meher. Then pointed

to the closet behind her.

Meher turned.

The closet door creaked open — but no one was there.

Except... there was something.

A torn scarf.

Bloodstained.

Her mother's scarf.

It smelled like lavender and something else.

Rust.

She collapsed to her knees, sobbing.

But the mirror-girl didn't flinch.

She smiled.

*"You gave her to me."*

Meher looked up. "Why?"

The mirror cracked.

And from its shattered silence, the answer whispered:

*"Because you asked me to."*

# CHAPTER TWENTY TWO

# The Silence Beneath

Ananya found Meher sitting on the floor, clutching a bloodstained scarf like it was the last thread tying her to sanity.

"Meher?" she whispered, stepping carefully into the room. The light was dim. The mirror... cracked.

Meher didn't look up. "She's not gone."

"Who?"

"The girl in the mirror."

Ananya froze.

There were footsteps above them — but the house had no upper floor.

She tried to laugh it off. "Meher, there's no one—"

"She knows your name too."

The mirror groaned. A sound like glass being dragged across bone.

Ananya turned to it.

The cracks had spread.

There were fingerprints on the *inside.*

"Meher, please," she said, voice shaking. "Let's go downstairs. This house is messing with us."

Meher looked at her then.

But her eyes didn't match.

They were darker. Hollow.

"No," she said softly. "It's not the house. It's *me.* I called her. I begged her to take the pain away. I thought she'd take the silence."

Ananya backed away. "You're scaring me."

"I'm scared too," Meher said. "But it's too late now. She's awake."

And then—

The mirror exploded.

Shards rained across the room.

Ananya screamed.

And Meher?

She stood still.

Blood trickled down her cheek where a shard had sliced it. But she didn't flinch.

She looked calm. Empty.

"The silence isn't mine anymore," she whispered. "It's *hers.*"

## CHAPTER TWENTY THREE

# Where The Light Doesn't Reach

Ananya barely remembered how they got out of that room.

All she knew was the mirror was gone, shattered into a hundred pieces, but something had stepped out of it — not in the way you'd see in horror movies, but in the way that fills the room with something wrong. Like the air had a weight, a voice, a grief too ancient to name.

Meher hadn't spoken since.

They sat at the bottom of the staircase, the walls too quiet, the silence pressing against their ears like cotton soaked in secrets.

Ananya finally asked, "Who did you call, Meher?"

Meher slowly raised her head. "Her name was whispered to me... in dreams. After Amma left."

Ananya's heart pounded. "You never told me your mom

died."
"She didn't. She *disappeared.* No note, no goodbye. Just... gone."
There was a long silence.
"I used to sit in that room," Meher said, voice breaking. "Every single night. Hoping she'd come back. I heard her voice. In the mirror. I thought it was her."
She looked at Ananya with eyes full of regret. "But it wasn't. I think I opened something I shouldn't have."
Thunder cracked outside. The lights flickered.
"I wanted silence to feel safe," Meher whispered. "But silence listens too closely. It hears your pain. And sometimes, it answers."
The room trembled — just slightly. Like the house was exhaling.
Ananya stood. "We have to leave."
But the front door wouldn't open.
The air grew colder.
On the wall opposite them, a message had appeared — as if traced by a fingertip in fog:
**"She was never yours to grieve."**
Ananya turned to Meher. "What does that mean?"
Meher's lips trembled. "I don't think Amma left. I think she was *taken.*"
And then they heard it.
A soft, lilting hum — coming from upstairs.
A lullaby.

The same one Meher used to hum in sleep.

## CHAPTER TWENTY FOUR

# The Song That Wasn't Meant For

The lullaby drifted down the staircase like smoke – gentle, almost beautiful. But in that beauty was something rotten. Meher froze.

"That's... Amma's lullaby," she whispered. "But she never sang it *like that*."

Ananya stepped closer to the stairs, her voice hushed. "Then who is singing it now?"

The hum floated in and out like a breath, echoing off the old wood panels. Ananya could feel it in her bones, vibrating through the banister under her hand.

They took slow steps up, every creak of the stairs sounding like a scream in the thick silence.

At the top, the hallway was darker than it had ever been — even in daylight. Shadows shifted in places where there should've been light.

Room by room, they searched, each door creaking open into emptiness.

And then Meher stopped at the end of the corridor.

Her mother's room.

The door was slightly open — just enough to see that the mirror inside was not reflecting anything anymore. Just black. Endless, swallowing black.

The lullaby stopped.

Ananya whispered, "Meher... wait."

But Meher had already pushed the door.

Inside, the mirror was alive. Not moving — but breathing. The glass rippled like water. And on the other side, a silhouette stood.

A woman.

Barefoot. Long braid. Sari draped loose like wind had forgotten to tuck it properly.

Her eyes were closed. But she was *weeping*.

"Amma..." Meher gasped.

The woman slowly lifted her head.

But it wasn't her.

The face was almost right. Almost soft. But too still. Too hollow. Like someone trying to wear her mother's grief as a mask.

And she spoke.

Not aloud. Inside them.

"You brought her back," the voice echoed through their skulls, cold and ancient. "But you never asked who I was first."

Meher stepped back. "You're not her. You never were."

"I was what you needed. A voice in the dark. A mother in your silence."

And the mirror began to crack. Slowly. From the corners inward.

"You invited me when you begged for her in tears."

Crack.

"You fed me with grief."

Crack.

"And now..."

Silence.

"*I want what you promised.*"

The mirror exploded.

## CHAPTER TWENTY FIVE

# Where Her Voice Went

Shards of glass flew out like knives, and Meher's instincts screamed too late. Ananya dragged her backward, shielding her from the rain of silver that sliced the air like it had been waiting years to break free.

The room groaned – not from wood or wind – but something alive. Something that had been asleep too long and was now wide awake.

Meher's breath hitched.

There, where the mirror had once hung, was not a wall – but a dark, narrow corridor. It wasn't supposed to exist. Not in the house blueprints, not in anyone's memory. But it was *there*, gaping and humming with a low sound like a thousand whispered regrets.

And on the wooden floor just before the passage: a photograph. Burnt at the edges. Faded.

Her mother. Smiling. Holding someone's hand.

Not her father's.

Ananya picked it up, lips parting in disbelief. "Meher... that's..."

Meher shook her head, her voice finally trembling through the silence. "No. That can't be real."

But it was.

Behind the photo, a diary page — the same handwriting she had spent years memorizing.

*They told me not to go back to the corridor. That if I opened it again, it wouldn't be just me who got lost. But Meher... she's still so small. If she hears me whispering to her at night, I hope she forgives me for what I've let in.*

The floor beneath them groaned again — this time like something shifting beneath the wood. Ananya turned toward the corridor. "This isn't just a secret, Meher. This is a trap."

The air inside the corridor was colder, not just temperature-wise — but emotionally. Like grief had been preserved here, layered and piled over the years, like blankets soaked in tears.

And then, the voice returned. Whispering.

Not from the mirror.

Not from the corridor.

From *inside* Meher's ears.

*You were never supposed to hear me. But you did. And*

*now, you can't ever forget me.*

She clasped her hands over her ears, but the voice just grew louder.

"You opened the silence," the voice hissed. "Now listen to what it hides."

Suddenly, the door behind them slammed shut.

They were locked in.

The corridor breathed them in.

## CHAPTER TWENTY SIX

# What Was Buried Beneath

The corridor stretched far longer than it should have. Every step they took echoed – not outward, but inward. As if the house was inhaling the sound of their presence and storing it deep in its bones.

The air thickened, like they were walking underwater. Paint peeled from the walls in thin, curled strands, and somewhere ahead, something dripped steadily... drip... drip... drip... as though time itself was bleeding.

Meher stopped. "Did you hear that?"

Ananya nodded silently.

It wasn't just water.

It was breathing.

Heavy. Wet. From behind the walls.

They turned a corner, and there it was – a door. Old, rotting. It hadn't been opened in decades, yet it trembled ever so slightly, like it was waiting.

Meher reached out.

Ananya gripped her wrist. "Are you sure?"

Meher didn't answer. Her silence was no longer fear — it was hunger. She needed to know. The truth had teased her for too long, played hide and seek in her dreams, whispered through cracks and glass and empty frames. She needed it to *end.*

The door creaked open.

The room smelled of old tears.

Inside was a desk. A dusty tape recorder. A shattered photo frame. Another diary, its pages open — the ink smeared by something too fresh to be age.

And in the corner... a figure.

Facing the wall.

Hair long, black, tangled like roots.

Ananya whispered, "Meher..."

The figure turned slowly — but not its body. Only its head.

And the eyes — the eyes — were hers.

Meher's.

She stumbled back, heart crashing inside her chest.

The figure whispered with her exact voice, "Why didn't you come sooner?"

Then it vanished. No scream. No puff of smoke.

Just *gone.*

The tape recorder clicked.

It began to play.

*If you found this, Meher... it means I couldn't hold it back. The silence was stronger than me. I tried to bury it inside this house, inside the mirrors, inside the walls. But you — my daughter — you were always meant to find it.*

*I'm sorry.*

*Forgive me.*

The voice was her mother's. But older. Shakier. Like it had been recorded the moment before a breakdown.

And then something banged above them — a soft thud.

And another.

Like footsteps.

On the ceiling.

Meher and Ananya looked up — and the ceiling split down the middle.

## CHAPTER TWENTY SEVEN

# The House That Remembered

The crack tore through the ceiling with a sound like ribs breaking. Dust rained down. A piece of the plaster dropped near Meher's foot, and with it came something else—thin, yellowed paper, folded and sealed with wax.

She picked it up.

The wax bore her mother's initials.

Ananya, pale as the moonlight slicing through the broken window, whispered, "Why is your mother's letter... inside the ceiling?"

Meher said nothing. She couldn't. Her throat had dried into stone. Her fingers trembled as she peeled the seal open. The letter smelled faintly of jasmine and something older... decay.

*Meher,*

*If you're reading this, then the house has chosen you.*

*This place—it's not just wood and bricks. It's memory. And every memory I ever tried to bury—every scream I didn't let out—every moment of silence I forced into your life—it grew inside these walls.*

*The house remembers Meher. It feeds on forgotten things.*

*And it wants you to remember too.*

Suddenly, the walls around them began to whisper.

Not loudly. Not angrily.

Just... whispering.

Her name.

*Meher... Meher... Meher...*

Hundreds of voices, murmuring all at once.

Some hers. Some of her mother's. Some unknown.

The mirrors on the walls began to fog from the inside. Not condensation—*breath.* As if something trapped behind the glass had suddenly started breathing.

Ananya grabbed her hand. "We need to get out."

But Meher didn't move. Her eyes were fixed on the staircase leading upward—the one that didn't exist in the house's floor plan. The one that had suddenly appeared, old and creaking, twisting up into shadow.

"There's something up there," she said.

Ananya shook her head. "No. There's nothing good left here."

Meher pulled her hand away.

"I need to see."

And with that, she stepped onto the first stair.

Each creak beneath her feet was a memory resurfacing.

A bedtime song. A slammed door. Her mother's voice saying *I'll be right back*—but never returning.

Halfway up, she turned back.

Ananya hadn't followed.

Because something had closed the door behind her.

And Meher was alone.

Alone with the past.

Alone with what the house was finally ready to show her.

# CHAPTER TWENTY EIGHT

# WHAT THE SILENCE HID

The stairs seemed endless, like they weren't built to reach a floor, but a memory—buried so deep, it hurt to breathe. With every step, Meher's legs grew heavier, her heart pounding so loud it drowned out the whispering walls.

At the top was a single door. Faded blue. Just like the one in her childhood home—the one to her mother's room. It shouldn't be here.

Her fingers hovered above the doorknob.

Then she heard it.

Humming.

A lullaby.

Her mother's lullaby.

*"Neend mein teri, sapne mere... chupke se aayenge..."*

Tears blurred Meher's eyes.

She turned the knob.

The door opened not to a room—but a memory.

A perfectly frozen evening.

A woman sat on the edge of the bed—her mother. But she looked... broken. Not the way Meher remembered, but tired, her hands shaking, her face pale and shadowed with something deeper than sadness.

There was a child in the corner.

Young Meher.

Curled up in silence.

Watching.

Always watching.

Meher stepped inside, unsure if she was intruding in someone else's pain or reliving her own.

Her mother didn't look up, but spoke softly, as if she knew Meher was there.

*"I didn't leave because I wanted to, Meher. I left because the house made me. Because the silence wasn't mine—it belonged to the house. I only tried to protect you from what it was hiding."*

The walls cracked. A violent tremble shook the floor. But Meher didn't flinch.

"I don't want to be protected anymore," she whispered. "I want the truth."

Her mother's figure looked up now. Her eyes—full of grief and love—met hers.

And then she vanished.

The room began collapsing. The walls peeled like skin, exposing something underneath—photographs, letters, scribbled notes, all pulsing like veins. A secret the house had buried beneath years of dust and silence.

Meher tried to pick up one photo, but it burned her fingers.

She screamed.

The house wasn't revealing the truth.

It was *forcing* her to *feel* it.

The silence hadn't just belonged to her mother.

It had been *passed down.*

Inherited.

Like a curse.

A legacy of unspoken words and hidden pain.

And Meher—

Meher was the final one to carry it.

The room exploded into light.

White.

Blinding.

Then—

Black.

## CHAPTER TWENTY NINE

# The Voice Beyond The Attic

The storm hadn't let up for three days. Rain slithered down the glass like veins, and thunder cracked the silence every few minutes, echoing like the sky itself was breaking open. Meher stood still in the hallway, her eyes fixed on the attic door above the staircase. It was open now. Not wide, but slightly—just enough to show the blackness behind it, like a slit in the ceiling of reality. That door hadn't been touched in years. It *shouldn't* have opened.

Her chest tightened with a feeling that had no name—like grief mixed with dread, like a scream held under water.

Ananya sat by the window, arms wrapped around her knees. Her eyes weren't just empty... they were *hollowed out.* She hadn't spoken since sunrise, when she pointed at the attic with trembling fingers and whispered, "It was open when I woke up."

No one else was in the house.

Meher's legs moved without permission. One step. Then another. The staircase moaned beneath her weight as if warning her not to go further. But something compelled her—curiosity, maybe. Or madness. Or that same pull she used to feel when her mother called her name before bedtime, years ago, soft and sweet. Only now, it sounded... *wrong*.

She reached the attic. The door groaned louder when she pushed it open. Inside was cold—unnaturally cold. Like it hadn't felt warmth in decades. Dust curled in the air like it was breathing. Every shadow looked like it could move. Every sound echoed too long.

And then she saw it.

A cassette player.

Old. Rusted. Wrapped in spiderwebs.

It clicked on by itself.

Meher froze.

The voice that came through wasn't just familiar. It was *impossible.*

"I didn't want to disappear. They made me."

Her mother's voice.

Her *dead* mother's voice.

Then a long pause. And then the sound of scratching.

*Like nails against wood. Like someone locked inside.*

Meher reached for the stop button.

But before she could touch it, a whisper—not from the cassette, but *right next to her ear*—cut through the silence, cold and sharp:

**"You're next."**

She stumbled back, heart thrashing. Her foot hit something soft. A *doll*, its eyes blacked out, its mouth stitched shut.

She hadn't brought it here.

And it was wearing her childhood dress.

## CHAPTER THIRTY

# The Thing That Knows Her Name

Meher didn't sleep. Couldn't.

The attic's silence was louder than the storm outside.

Her mother's voice—*that voice*—still echoed in her skull like a curse that wouldn't fade. Ananya hadn't left the window all night. She just stared at the rain as though it were bleeding from the sky.

At 3:07 AM, the power went out.

Not flickered.

Gone.

Total black.

Meher reached for the torch beside her bed, but it wasn't there. Only cold sheets and something else—*fabric.* Rough. Damp. She pulled it out from under the pillow.

It was a hospital gown.

Her mother's hospital gown.

And it smelled like the lake.

She stumbled back, breathing sharp and fast, when her phone buzzed. A message from an unknown number.

**"It's not over. Come to the place she drowned."**

But her mother didn't drown.

*Did she?*

The message vanished.

She stared at the screen, now black, now useless. A crack formed across the glass, slowly, like something pressed from the inside.

Then the door creaked open.

Nobody there.

But the hall was filled with muddy footprints. *Small ones.* Barefoot. Leading from the front door... to her room.

She followed them with her eyes, heart hammering, skin cold.

Until she saw it.

Written on the mirror in red—not blood. Something darker.

**"You forgot what you did."**

And underneath, in a smaller, shakier hand:

**"But I didn't."**

## CHAPTER THIRTY ONE

# The Lake Remembers

The town's lake was still, unnaturally still, like it had made a pact with the night to not give anything away. Meher stood at the edge, Ananya a step behind her, flashlight trembling in her hand. Fog slithered across the surface like it was alive, hiding whatever truth lay beneath.

Neither of them spoke.

Neither wanted to break whatever terrible silence had settled.

Meher knelt near the shoreline, her fingers tracing the patterns of mud that matched the same footprints from her hallway. They ended right there. At the water. Like someone had walked straight in and vanished.

She looked at Ananya. "Are you sure you saw her?"

Ananya nodded. Slowly. Hesitantly. "It was her face.

But... not her eyes."
A shiver crawled down Meher's spine.
Something wasn't right with the lake. It didn't feel like water anymore. It felt like glass. Like if she leaned over, she'd see not her reflection—but someone else's. And deep down, she didn't want to know whose.
Then came the whisper.
Not from the trees. Not from the wind. From *below.*
Bubbling up like air escaping lungs underwater.
**"Meherrrrr..."**
The voice curled around her like smoke. Familiar. Sweet. Rotting.
Ananya screamed and pointed toward the water. Meher turned—
And froze.
A pale face hovered just below the surface.
Eyes wide.
Mouth open in a silent scream.
Hair floating like seaweed, tangled with what looked like hospital bracelets and broken bangles.
Meher staggered back, falling into Ananya, who caught her, trembling just as hard. But when they looked again... the lake was empty. Just ripples. Just silence. Just... waiting.
Then, Meher's phone rang.
Her mother's name on the screen.
And when she answered, all she heard was her own

voice.

**"I know what you did."**

## CHAPTER THIRTY TWO

# THE DIARY UNDER THE FLOORBOARDS

Meher didn't sleep that night.

Every creak of the house was louder. Every shadow deeper. Every thought darker.

She couldn't get the lake out of her mind. That *face*. That call from her *mother's name*, but in her *own voice*.

Something was wrong—so deeply, dreadfully wrong.

Her fingers twitched with anxiety as she sat on the cold floor of her mother's abandoned room. She hadn't stepped in there since the night everything changed. But now, something kept pulling her back. Like the house itself wanted her to see something.

She sat in silence, letting the room breathe around her.

Then... *creak.*

The floorboard beneath her shifted.

Meher froze.

She slowly got to her knees and pressed on it. Another creak. Another tiny shift. Her heart started racing. She pulled the carpet back, hands shaking. The wood below was cracked—almost deliberately loosened.

Digging her fingers in, she pried it open.

Beneath it was a dusty, leather-bound book, stained and faded—its edges eaten slightly by time, or maybe something else. She stared at it, hesitant to touch. But her hands moved anyway.

It was a diary.

Her mother's.

She opened it carefully.

And that's when the air in the room shifted.

The first page wasn't dated. It simply read:

"If you are reading this, I'm probably already gone. And it wasn't an accident."

Meher's breath hitched.

"They think I don't remember what happened that night. But I do. Every second. Every scream. Every lie they forced me to believe."

The pages trembled in her hands.

"I saw something at the lake. I saw **her**."

And then—*thump*.

From the hallway.

Another *thump*.

Slow. Deliberate. Heavy.

Meher's blood ran cold.

She closed the diary.

*Thump.*

Something—or someone—was walking toward the room.

The floor creaked.

The door handle twisted.

Meher couldn't move. Couldn't breathe.

And just as the door inched open, revealing a sliver of darkness—

The candle beside her blew out.

## CHAPTER THIRTY THREE

# The Things That Watch In Silence

She didn't scream.

She couldn't.

Meher sat frozen in the pitch dark, the diary clutched to her chest like a shield against whatever had just opened the door. But when she looked—nothing. No footsteps. No figure. Just cold air seeping into her skin like frostbite.

She lit the candle again, her hands trembling. Its weak flame flickered violently, casting jagged shadows across the room like dancing ghosts.

She should've run. She should've burned the book. But something kept her grounded—some horrible need to know.

She opened the next page.

"I wasn't supposed to find the photos. But I did. Buried

behind the wardrobe. Meher was just six. She doesn't remember. But *I do.* I know who the girl in the picture was."

"Her name was Ananya. And she wasn't *alive* when that photo was taken."

Meher's pulse slammed in her ears.

Ananya.

The same girl from her nightmares.

The name whispered in the forest.

The voice that called from the lake.

She turned the next page.

And a photograph slid out.

It was old. Water-damaged. But clear enough to make her heart collapse.

A little girl—wearing *Meher's exact face.*

Standing beside a woman with hollow eyes.

Behind them, a man with no face. His head was blurred.

As if he moved too fast for the photo to catch him.

Or... like he didn't belong there.

And written in crooked ink on the back—

*"The one who watches. The one who waits. Don't let her look in the mirror too long."*

Meher dropped the photo.

And behind her—*a soft laugh.* A girl's laugh.

Then a whisper, close, *right by her ear.*

"You remember me now, don't you?"

She spun around.

Nothing.

But in the mirror across the room, her reflection smiled.

And *she hadn't moved her lips.*

## CHAPTER THIRTY FOUR

# Not All Mirrors Reflect You

The mirror was wrong.

Meher stood rooted, heart banging like fists against her chest. Her reflection stood still—grinning, head tilted ever so slightly to the left.

But Meher wasn't smiling.

She took a step back.

The reflection didn't.

She reached out slowly, almost hoping this was just sleep-deprived madness. That her mind had finally fractured under grief, trauma, and whatever this place was.

But when she touched the glass—

—it was *warm*.

Breathing.

Like skin.

The reflection moved then. But not like her. It raised a hand and tapped gently on the other side of the glass, eyes dark as tunnels. And as it leaned closer, the smile widened—impossibly, painfully wide.

"You're in *my* place, Meher. You were never supposed to stay this long."

She backed away, shaking, clutching her diary like a crucifix. Her legs felt like melting wax. She turned and ran from the room, slamming the door behind her.

But the mirror's giggle followed her down the hall.

She sprinted to the kitchen, her thoughts chaotic. Who *was* Ananya? Why did she look exactly like her? Why did that photo exist before she was even born?

And why did her mother's handwriting in the diary slowly start to look... like her own?

The phone. She needed to call someone. Anyone.

She grabbed the old landline. Static.

Then a voice.

"You can't call the dead, sweetheart."

Click.

She screamed, flinging the receiver across the room.

And then the house went *silent*. Not empty—just *too* quiet. As if it were holding its breath.

And in that stillness, Meher realized something chilling.

There were no photos of her past in this house. None of her birthdays. None of her childhood.

Only the same girl in different clothes.

Ananya.

And in every one—Ananya was standing in *Meher's room.*

Sleeping in *Meher's bed.*

Wearing *Meher's face.*

## CHAPTER THIRTY FIVE

# The House That Has Everything

Meher packed in a frenzy. She didn't care where she would go, she just had to leave. Her fingers trembled as she zipped up her bag, breathing fast, trying to convince herself that all of this—every shadow, every whisper, every face that wasn't hers in the mirror—was just in her head. A trick. A prolonged nightmare.

But the house... it was *watching* her.

Every creak on the staircase. Every blink of the hallway light. It was like the walls themselves were leaning in, listening, remembering.

She reached the front door, hand on the knob.

Locked.

She hadn't locked it. She was sure she hadn't.

She turned it again.

*Still locked.*

Then, from behind her, a quiet, childlike hum floated through the air—the same lullaby her mother used to sing when she was scared.

Her bag dropped.

"Who's there?" she whispered, voice cracking.

Silence.

She turned back, her breath hitching as the hallway behind her stretched longer, darker, deeper—like it wasn't a hallway anymore. Like it was *pulling her back in.*

"Stop it," she whispered. "You're not real. This isn't real."

But then came the soft sound of footsteps. Small. Barefoot. Slow. Coming toward her from the shadows.

And then a whisper, not in her ear—but in her *head*:

"You think you're leaving, Meher? You never even arrived."

The hallway lights blew out in one loud *crack.*

And the house laughed—low and broken, like wood splitting under pressure. She fell to her knees, sobbing, not just from fear but from a deep, guttural sorrow she couldn't name. She missed her mother. But... did she even have one?

She crawled to the edge of the wall, trembling.

And found it.

A photograph. Burned at the edges, lying hidden beneath the floorboards.

Her mother.

Holding a baby.
Only… the baby's face was scratched out.
And written behind it, in faded ink:
*"If she ever remembers—take her back."*

# CHAPTER THIRTY SIX

# The Corridor Below

The floorboard creaked beneath her fingers, and before she could even think, it gave way.

Meher fell through the splintering wood, her scream swallowed by the pitch-black descent. She landed hard, her shoulder scraping against stone. Darkness wrapped around her like a second skin. No light. No sound. Just her heartbeat—loud and fast and scared.

She got up slowly, her fingers brushing against the wall. It was damp.

And breathing.

Yes, breathing. In and out. Slow, like the house had lungs and she was trapped inside it.

There was only one direction to go—forward. A narrow stone corridor stretched endlessly ahead, lit faintly by flickering lanterns nailed into the wall. They weren't

there before. But they were now.
Meher walked, her legs trembling, shadows dancing on both sides. The deeper she went, the more the air felt heavy. Like grief. Like memory.
Then, she saw it—etched into the stone wall.
"She should've stayed quiet."
It was written in what looked like rust. Or maybe something darker.
With every step, the whispers began to return.
But they weren't in her voice anymore.
They were her *mother's.*
Sobbing. Pleading.
"Don't take her. Please. She's just a child..."
"I didn't tell her anything. I swear—"
"Leave her alone!"
Meher's chest tightened. The air turned ice-cold. She reached a door at the end of the corridor. Old. Wooden. Covered in handprints—some small, some large, all smudged into the wood like people had clawed to escape.
She pushed it open.
Inside was a room full of mirrors.
And in every single one—
She wasn't alone.
There were people. Faces. All distorted. Familiar.
And one—standing right behind her.
She turned, but no one was there.
When she looked back at the mirror, *her own reflection*

*was gone.*

## CHAPTER THIRTY SEVEN

# Reflections That Breathe

Meher's breath caught in her throat.

The mirror showed nothing—no reflection, no girl, just the room behind her. Her hands were shaking now, the kind of trembling that starts in the bones. She stepped closer to the glass. Her fingers hovered inches from it, heart hammering like a warning. Something was wrong. Very wrong.

Then the mirror **breathed.**

Fog bloomed across the glass, like a cold exhale from something inside. And written in that breath, slowly, painfully, was a name:

**"Meher."**

The letters bled downward.

She stumbled back—but the moment she did, all the other mirrors lit up.

One by one, they began showing her memories—**not her own**, but her mother's.
Her mother running through the house, dragging Meher as a child, hiding her beneath the staircase.
Her mother screaming behind a locked door.
Her mother standing in that same corridor, alone.
Crying.
And then—something dragging her mother away.
Something with hands too long. Fingers too many.
The real Meher screamed.
The mirrors cracked.
Every one of them **shattered inward**, like something inside had been watching—and had enough.
From the fragments, black liquid began to ooze out.
Thick. Slow. Alive.
And then she heard her mother's voice, crystal clear now, echoing all around:
"He's still here. And he never forgot."
The lanterns all went out at once.
Meher was swallowed in pitch-black silence.
And then...
A whisper, right next to her ear:
**"You were never supposed to come back."**

## CHAPTER THIRTY EIGHT

# THE MAN WITH NO EYES

The corridor was no longer quiet.

It was breathing.

The air had grown heavy, pressing against Meher's chest like invisible hands. Her ears were ringing, but beneath that, she heard it—a slow, dragging shuffle coming from the far end of the hallway. She tried to move, but her feet felt nailed to the ground. Then the lantern flickered on again, dimmer now, as though it too was afraid.

And she saw him.

Tall. Thin. Face shrouded in shadow. But what she could see made her blood freeze.

He had **no eyes**. Just two hollow sockets, deep and endless, leaking something black and thick, like ink. His lips were sewn shut. Not neatly. The thread was jagged, raw. Like someone wanted to keep his screams inside

forever.
Meher couldn't breathe. She couldn't even scream.
He lifted one trembling hand and pointed to her. His hand was shaking not from weakness—but from fury.
"Why did you come back?" a voice hissed—not from him, but **through the walls**, the floor, the air itself.
Then the corridor changed.
It stretched longer behind him, shadows multiplying like reflections in a broken mirror. And in each shadow—her mother. Standing. Crying. Mouth open. But... not calling for help.
They were warning her.
**Leave.**
The man took a step closer. And as his foot hit the ground, the house **moaned**, low and guttural.
Meher turned to run—but the corridor behind her was gone. It was now a wall of mirrors. And in every mirror was a reflection of her, looking more broken, more decayed, more lost.
This place was **not just haunted**.
It was feeding.
And she was next.

## CHAPTER THIRTY NINE

# The Hollow Ones

The silence after the whisper was not just silence—it was thick, humming, almost alive. Meher didn't dare breathe. Every sound felt amplified: her heartbeat, the groan of wood beneath her feet, the ticking that wasn't coming from any clock she could see. The mirrors lay shattered around her, but their reflections... they hadn't stopped. In each shard, something moved.

Not her. Not her mother.

Others.

Faceless. Hollow-eyed. Shadows that twitched with jerky, unnatural rhythm. Their heads turned toward her, all at once. A silent scream echoed across the glass, cracking the shards even further.

Meher ran.

She didn't know where she was going anymore. The house twisted in ways that no house should. Doors led to walls. Staircases to nowhere. Windows opened into pitch-black voids.

But the ticking—it kept getting louder.

And now, it was accompanied by whispers.

Voices layered over each other, thousands of them, speaking in fragmented pieces:

"*She was the last...*"

"*You opened it again...*"

"*The Hollow Ones remember...*"

"*You were meant to forget...*"

She slammed into a door she didn't know existed. It creaked open with a sound like bones snapping.

Inside was a nursery.

Her old one.

But it wasn't how she remembered. The crib was overturned, claw marks scarred the walls, and the mobile above the ceiling spun furiously though there was no wind.

In the corner, something sat.

No face.

No body.

Just a shifting silhouette of darkness, like a child made from smoke and teeth.

It turned its head toward her.

"You left us," it said in her voice.

And then it crawled.

Not walked—**crawled**, in jerks and spasms, like it didn't quite know how to be human.

Meher screamed.

She slammed the door shut just as it reached her, its long fingers brushing her ankle.

She ran again.

But now, the whispers followed her.

And she realized—

They were never coming from the house.

They were coming from **inside her.**

## CHAPTER FORTY

# Trapped In The Frame

The house didn't breathe anymore.

It *watched.*

Meher could feel it in the stillness—as if every wall, every shadow, had turned to listen. Her feet pressed softly on the rotting floorboards as she entered the basement again, this time without Ananya. This time alone.

The stairs creaked louder than before, like they remembered her weight.

In her trembling hands, she held the camera. Not to take another picture—but because it had started clicking on its own again. Once. Then again. Every time she stepped closer to the center of the room, the lens twitched.

Click.

Click.

Click.

The mirror in the basement hadn't been there before. Not the last time. But now it stood—tall, cracked at the center, as if something had once tried to escape from inside it.

And just behind her reflection, stood a figure.

Not moving.

Not breathing.

But waiting.

Meher turned sharply—nothing.

She turned back. The figure was gone.

Her camera slipped from her hands and hit the floor. But it kept clicking.

And when she picked it up, the screen showed an image it had just taken:

Her.

And behind her... a hallway that didn't exist in the real world.

A hallway filled with faces—mouths open. Screaming.

She looked around. No hallway. No faces.

But when she touched the screen, the image moved.

The hallway *pulled her in.*

And Meher realized the truth.

The camera didn't *capture* memories.

It *trapped* them.

## CHAPTER FORTY ONE

# The Clicking Never Stops

The camera was gone.

Meher had placed it on her desk—right there, by the window where the light used to feel safe. But now, the space was empty. Just cold wood and the faint, sticky trace of something that smelled like iron and rot.

She didn't scream. She couldn't.

Because the photos on her wall—the ones she never put up—were changing.

Each of them.

The one of Ananya laughing under the tree now showed her standing behind Meher in the corridor... eyes blacked out.

The one of the school building was now burnt. Smoke curled in the frame, as if the photo itself had caught fire and frozen mid-moment.

The photo of her mother—the only one she still had—was fading. Her face slowly vanishing. As if someone was erasing her memory from existence.

Click.

She froze.

That sound.

It wasn't in her head.

Click.

It came again. Closer. Behind her.

Click.

She turned.

No one was there.

But the Polaroids had multiplied. Crawled up the wall. Dozens, maybe hundreds. Some were upside down, others torn, some completely black. All of them watching.

The last photo dropped from the ceiling.

It fluttered down like a dying leaf and landed at Meher's feet.

She picked it up with shaking hands.

It was a picture of her. Taken just seconds ago.

And right behind her in the photo—

A figure. Featureless. Tall. Standing in the shadows of her room.

She didn't dare turn around.

The camera clicked again.

But this time...

It wasn't from the desk.
It was in her hands.
And her fingers weren't on the shutter.

## CHAPTER FORTY TWO

# GHOST IN THE LENS

The air inside the attic was still, but not the kind of stillness that brought calm. It was the kind that screamed silence—unnatural, heavy, like the air itself was waiting for something. Meher stepped inside slowly, the floor groaning beneath her feet. Ananya followed, her fingers clutching the strap of the old camera like it was her only anchor.

The room was filled with broken toys, rusted mirrors, and old wooden mannequins—each of them headless.

The moment Meher's foot crossed the threshold, the attic door slammed shut behind them with a bang.

They froze.

Then came the whispering. Low at first, like wind threading through cracks in the wood, but it began to rise—layered, voices stacked on voices. Meher couldn't make out the words, but she knew they were calling *her name.*

She turned to Ananya—but her friend wasn't looking at her.

She was looking at the far end of the attic.

Where the mannequins were beginning to move.

Not all at once. One twitching finger here. One rotating neck there. Except... they had no heads. No eyes. No faces. And still, they turned toward Meher, as though they *knew* her.

The whispering got louder.

One of them took a step forward.

Meher backed away until her spine hit the wall. "This isn't real," she muttered.

But Ananya was shaking too. "They're *hollow*, Meher. The ones who were taken... they come back like this."

"Taken by what?"

"The man with no eyes," she whispered.

Meher's breath hitched.

The room began to grow colder, breath visible now. She looked into the nearest mirror, cracked and blackened—and saw not her reflection, but *a tall figure*, eyeless, skin stretched thin over a skull-like face, standing behind her.

She spun around.

Nothing.

But the mannequins were closer now.

Much closer.

Their limbs bending in impossible angles, they creaked forward as if pulled by something unseen. One reached out—and Meher screamed.

Ananya yanked her toward the door, which refused to open. She kicked it. Pounded on it.

And then… they heard the voice.

Not from outside.

Not from inside.

But from *within* Meher's own ears.

"He's waiting, Meher. And you brought her right to him."

## CHAPTER FORTY THREE

# The Silence That Screamed

The door shut behind her without a sound. Meher stood alone in the final corridor of the house, and it felt like the house had been waiting for her all along. The air was unnaturally still, yet thick with something unsaid, like the breath of the house was caught in its throat. She took a step forward. The floor groaned—not from her weight, but like it remembered.

The walls here were different. They weren't lined with mirrors or portraits or bloodstained wallpaper. No, this place was bare. A silence lived here, loud and cruel, humming with something ancient. The lantern in her hand flickered, and then all at once, it went out.

Darkness swallowed everything.

She fumbled, heart hammering, when a low hum began. Not music. Not a whisper. Something between—a chant of the forgotten. And then came the scraping.

Not footsteps.

Fingers.

Long, sharp, claw-like fingers dragging themselves along the walls, circling her. She pressed herself against the cold stone, trying not to breathe. A shadow moved ahead —then another. And then she saw him.

The man with no eyes.

He was taller than memory. Hollow where his eyes should've been. And this time, he wasn't a memory. He was here. He was *real.* He smiled, cracked and bleeding at the edges, and lifted a hand to his face. From his eyeless sockets, a stream of thick black tears poured.

"Why did you come back, Meher?" he asked. But it wasn't his voice.

It was her mother's.

Meher stepped back, tears stinging her eyes. "Where is she?" she choked.

He tilted his head. "She gave herself to the house. So you wouldn't have to."

And suddenly the walls cracked open—not crumbled, not shattered—they *opened,* like mouths. And inside them were eyes. Watching. All of them. Hundreds. Red. Wet. Alive.

Memories bled from the cracks.

Her mother screaming.

Ananya's voice whispering, *Don't trust the house,*

*Meher.*

And then her own voice: *What if I was never meant to leave?*

The floor beneath her gave way. She fell—not through space, but through memories. Each one darker. Bloodier. Until she landed with a gasp—on a cold floor, in a room she had never seen.

Except she had.

She was in the photograph. The one with the blurred man in the corner.

And this time, she wasn't holding the camera.

He was.

And he clicked.

The flash blinded her.

The last thing she saw before darkness again was her mother's reflection—in the corner, crying.

And then silence. But this time, it *screamed.*

# CHAPTER FORTY FOUR

# The Last Room On The Left

The hallway felt endless.

Each step Meher took echoed behind her, louder than the one before, as though the walls themselves were listening. The light from her lantern flickered with every breath she took, shadows melting across the faded wallpaper like ink in water. Ananya walked beside her, silent now, her face pale, eyes sunken from the horror they had just seen. Neither of them spoke. Words were too fragile here. They would only shatter under the weight of what they now knew.

The house was not just haunted.

It remembered.

It remembered *everything.*

And it was leading them—guiding them—to the place where it had all ended.

Meher's hand brushed the wall, fingers tracing the dents and cracks, the torn edges of pictures long removed. As they passed by a room on the right, the door opened on its own with a long, aching groan. She peeked inside—just for a second—and saw a crib.

Empty.

But swaying.

She didn't stop to look further. She couldn't. Not now.

Ahead, at the very end of the corridor, a single door stood slightly ajar. It hadn't been there before. It was as though the house had *grown* it.

The last room on the left.

Meher's steps slowed.

Her fingers trembled as she reached for the doorknob. It was cold—ice cold. The kind of cold that burned. She turned it anyway. The door creaked open slowly, revealing a small, dust-covered room. A rocking chair sat in the corner, still moving, though no one had touched it.

And there, on the far wall, was a mirror.

Shattered.

Meher stepped inside, her heartbeat a drum in her ears.

On the ground sat an old tape recorder.

She didn't know why, but she bent down and pressed play.

A crackle of static.

Then her mother's voice.

Soft. Breaking.

> “If someone finds this… please know I tried. I tried to protect her. I locked the memories away, I sealed the doors, I burned what I could. But he’s still here. Watching. Waiting. And I don’t think… I don’t think I’ll make it.”

Meher’s throat tightened.

> “Tell her I love her. Tell her not to come back here. Tell her—”

The tape clicked off.

Meher stood frozen, her chest rising and falling with quiet sobs. Her hands balled into fists. The pain—sharp and deep—spiked through her ribs like something was trying to crawl out from her past.

Ananya whispered, “Meher… we shouldn’t be here.”

But Meher wasn’t listening.

Because she had finally seen what lay beneath the broken mirror.

A photograph.

Black and white.

Of her mother.

Standing in this same room.

Holding Meher.

And behind them…

That same faceless man.

Watching.

## CHAPTER FORTY FIVE

# The Girl In The Photograph

The photograph slipped from Meher's fingers, landing face-down on the dusty floor with a whisper.

She didn't move.

She couldn't.

Her eyes were fixed on the empty space where her reflection *should* have been.

It was gone.

Not flickering.

Not fading.

Gone.

Ananya called her name again. But it was distant. Hollow. Like it was coming from another world.

The photo... she had to look again.

She picked it up slowly, dread pooling in her stomach like ice.

There it was—her mother, holding a girl in her lap.

But it wasn't her.

She knew it now.

That child's eyes were wide and bright. A chipped front tooth. Dressed in a pale pink frock she never owned.

At the back of the photo, scribbled in clumsy, rushed handwriting:

**"To Meher. My daughter. My forgiveness."**

Her chest clenched.

What did that mean?

Then the diary entries flooded her mind again—each one about **losing** Meher, about **grief**, about **making it right**.

But not once... not once... had they described *her*.

Because *she* wasn't the girl being mourned.

She was the mistake.

She was the *replacement*.

Suddenly, the glass around the room shattered inward.

The mirror before her flickered—and now, her reflection returned.

But it wasn't mirroring her.

It smiled when she didn't.

It tilted its head in the opposite direction.

And then, it stepped forward—*out of the mirror*.

It looked just like her.

Same eyes. Same voice.

But colder.

Older.

Angrier.

> "You're not Meher," it whispered.

She backed away.

"No... I am. I grew up here. I remember the house. I remember her—"

> "You were made to remember. Planted memories. Built lies. She made you."

Ananya screamed behind her, but Meher didn't turn.

Couldn't.

Everything around her warped. The house sighed like it was tired of pretending.

She wasn't *in* a haunted house.

She *was* the haunting.

The house hadn't remembered her.

It had **recognized what she wasn't.**

And then came the final blow.

The figure before her—the girl who looked like her—held something in her hand.

A birth certificate.

It read:

**Name: Meher Rao**

**Date of Death: 12th July, 2017**

**Cause: Drowned – foul play suspected**

And then she spoke again.

But this time... the voice was different.

It wasn't the ghost.

It wasn't the house.

It was *her own voice*, recorded.

Crackling through an old tape player in the corner:

> "If you're hearing this... then it means I've failed.
>
> I wasn't supposed to remember.
>
> I was built to forget.
>
> But memories don't die.
>
> And neither do ghosts."

Meher fell to her knees.

Because it wasn't her story.

It was never hers.

She wasn't the haunted girl.

She was the **ghost that replaced her**.

Fabricated.

Programmed.

Loved by a grieving mother who couldn't let go.

A memory so strong, it became real.

But never *truly* alive.

Ananya tried to touch her—and her hand went straight through.

No warmth.

No skin.

No *Meher*.

And then... the lights faded.

One by one.

The diary caught fire on its own.

The last thing she saw was her mother, in the hallway.

Smiling, as if she was finally letting go.

Because the real Meher... had finally come home.

And the shadow pretending to be her?

She was no longer needed.

She looked down at her hands one last time.

They were fading.

She whispered something into the dark.

No one would ever hear it.

But if they did, it would've sounded like:

> "I just wanted to be loved."

And then—

She vanished.

Like she was never real at all.

9 789370 923034

Printed by Libri Plureos GmbH in Hamburg, Germany